LE HAVRE TRAVEL GUIDE 2023 & BEYOND:

Your Ultimate Travel Companion to Immerse Yourself in Elegance, Heritage, and Adventure, and Discover the Charms of Normandy's Coastal Gem.

Greene Annabella

Copyright © 2023 by Greene Annabella

All rights reserved. No part of this publication may be reproduced, stored in a retrieval system, or transmitted, in any form or by any means, electronic, mechanical, photocopying, recording, or otherwise, without the prior written permission of the publisher, except for brief quotations in critical reviews or articles.

This book is sold subject to the condition that it shall not, by way of trade or otherwise, be lent, re-sold, hired out, or otherwise circulated without the publisher's prior consent in any form of binding or cover other than that in which it is published and without a similar condition including this condition being imposed on the subsequent purchaser.

Table of Content

INTRODUCTION **4**
   My Le Havre Story 4
   An Overview of it's Splendor and Significance 8

CHAPTER 1: Planning Your Trip **13**
   When to Visit: Best Seasons and Events 13
   Packing List for your adventure 16
   Practical Information: Travel Essentials and Local Tips.. 21
   Transportation Options: Getting to and Around Le Havre 26

CHAPTER 2: Unveiling Le Havre's Essence **31**
   The History of Le Havre: From Past to Present 31
   Architectural Marvels: Exploring the City's Unique Structures 34
   Art and Culture: Museums, Galleries, and Cultural Highlights 39

CHAPTER 3: Coastal Charm and Scenic Splendor ... 46
   The Seaside Beauty: Beaches and Seascapes 46
   Strolling Along the Promenade: Beachfront Activities... 50
   Day Trips to Nearby Coastal Wonders 53

CHAPTER 4: Culinary Delights and Gastronomic Adventures **59**
   A Taste of Normandy: Local Cuisine and Specialties .. 59
   Dining Options: Restaurants, Cafes, and Food Markets.

63

Wine and Dine: Pairing Your Meals with Local Wines 67

CHAPTER 5: Elegance and Entertainment..................72

Shopping in Style: Boutiques, Souvenirs, and Local Crafts.. 72

Nightlife and Entertainment: Bars, Theatres, and Evening Activities..76

Events and Festivals: Immersing Yourself in Local Celebrations..80

CHAPTER 6: Outdoor Pursuits and Adventure....... 84

Exploring Nature: Parks, Gardens, and Outdoor Recreation..84

Sports and Activities: Surfing, Sailing, and More........ 88

Thrilling Adventures: Excursions Beyond the City Limits.. 91

CHAPTER 7: Practicalities for a Smooth Journey.... 94

Accommodation Options: Hotels, B&Bs, and Rentals... 94

Health and Safety: Tips for a Secure and Healthy Stay.... 99

CHAPTER 8: Beyond Le Havre: Exploring Normandy 104

Day Trips to Nearby Towns and Villages................... 104

Exploring the Normandy Countryside: Landmarks and Natural Beauty.. 106

Basic phrases... 111

CONCLUSION...113

BONUS: Travel Journal.. 117

3

INTRODUCTION

My Le Havre Story

In the midst of bustling cities and serene landscapes, there exists a gem on the coastline of Normandy, a place that beckons travelers with its maritime allure and cultural riches—Le Havre. As I ventured into this coastal haven, little did I know that my journey would be a tapestry woven with elegance, heritage, and adventure.

Upon arriving in Le Havre, I was immediately captivated by the marriage of modernity and history that graced the city's streets. The towering spires of St. Joseph's Church stood in stark contrast to the sleek lines of contemporary buildings, a testament to Le Havre's resilience after its post-World War II reconstruction. As I meandered through the city, I marveled at the fusion of architectural styles, which narrated a tale of rebirth and innovation.

The city's artistry extended beyond buildings; it was etched into the very fabric of Le Havre. The Musée d'Art Moderne André Malraux, fondly known as MuMa, held within its walls a treasure trove of artistic brilliance. Walking through its galleries, I felt the strokes of impressionist masterpieces brush against my imagination, whispering stories of Monet and Boudin, who found inspiration in these very shores.

Le Havre's coastline, a dynamic dance between the land and sea, proved irresistible. The shores were adorned with inviting promenades and vibrant beaches that seemed to stretch to infinity. As I strolled along the water's edge, the salty breeze played with my hair, and the rhythmic sound of the waves became a comforting symphony. With the sea as my guide, I embarked on a maritime adventure aboard a traditional fishing boat. The gentle rocking of the vessel and the tales of seasoned fishermen painted a vivid picture of the sea's symbiotic relationship with the people of Le Havre.

Culinary escapades awaited, and Le Havre's gastronomic scene was a sensory odyssey. I savored the taste of creamy Camembert and briny oysters, each bite a tribute to Normandy's rich culinary heritage. The city's markets were a vibrant tapestry of colors and aromas, where locals passionately shared their produce and secrets to creating culinary delights. Under the warm glow of a charming bistro, I relished in conversations over glasses of Calvados, immersing myself in the joie de vivre that defines French culture.

Le Havre, however, wasn't just a city—it was a stage for cultural performances and enchanting encounters. As the sun dipped below the horizon, the city came alive with theater productions, street performances, and concerts. The passion of the performers and the cheers of the audience created an atmosphere of unison, where language barriers faded and emotions spoke a universal tongue.

Beyond the city's confines, nature beckoned with open arms. I embarked on a journey to the cliffs of Étretat, a short distance away, where nature had sculpted the landscape into breathtaking forms. Standing atop the cliffs, gazing out at the endless expanse of sea, I felt both humbled and invigorated by the power of the elements. The scenic beauty was a reminder that while Le Havre embraced modernity, it remained deeply connected to the natural world that surrounded it.

As my time in Le Havre drew to a close, I reflected on the memories I had woven into its tapestry. Each street corner, each bite of delicacy, and each wave that had brushed against the shore had left an indelible mark on my heart. Le Havre was more than a destination; it was an experience—a journey that had taught me the value of resilience, the beauty of diversity, and the magic of embracing both history and progress.

Leaving Le Havre wasn't a farewell; it was an au revoir, a promise to return and immerse myself in its elegance, heritage, and adventure once again. And as I watched the city's skyline disappear from view, I knew that the memories of this coastal haven would forever be etched into the mosaic of my life's adventures.

An Overview of it's Splendor and Significance

Le Havre, a coastal gem nestled in the heart of Normandy, France, stands as a testament to the harmonious blend of elegance, heritage, and adventure. This city, which emerged from the ashes of World War II with renewed vigor, carries within its streets and landscapes a rich tapestry of history and modernity, making it a destination of both splendor and significance.

The history of Le Havre is a story of resilience and rebirth. Following the devastating impacts of World War II, the city underwent a remarkable transformation. The reconstruction efforts led by architect Auguste Perret resulted in a unique architectural landscape that seamlessly merged modern design with the remnants of a storied past. The city's inclusion as a UNESCO World Heritage Site underscores its role as a living museum, showcasing the evolution of architectural styles and the triumph of human spirit over adversity.

Le Havre's significance extends beyond its physical transformation. It is a cultural hub where art, history, and innovation converge. The Musée d'Art Moderne André Malraux (MuMa) is a cultural beacon, housing an extensive collection of impressionist masterpieces that encapsulate the spirit of creativity that permeates the city. As visitors walk through its galleries, they are transported into the world of Monet, Boudin, and other luminaries who found inspiration in Le Havre's scenic beauty.

The city's allure is inexorably linked to its coastal charm. With a picturesque shoreline stretching as far as the eye can see, Le Havre offers a haven for those seeking solace by the sea. Its beaches, promenades, and marinas invite travelers to bask in the tranquil symphony of waves and seabirds, providing a canvas for relaxation and rejuvenation. And beyond the gentle lull of the tide lies the city's maritime legacy, as fishing boats and ships narrate tales of adventure and exploration.

Culinary enthusiasts find themselves captivated by Le Havre's gastronomic offerings. Normandy's renowned culinary traditions come to life in the city's markets, bistros, and eateries. From savory Camembert cheese to succulent seafood plucked fresh from the sea, every dish is a celebration of the region's bounty. Dining in Le Havre is an invitation to savor the flavors of the land and sea, an experience that transcends nourishment to become a journey of the senses.

Le Havre's vibrancy extends to its cultural festivities and entertainment. The city's events calendar is a vibrant tapestry of theater, music, and celebrations. The annual Festival de la Mer invites locals and visitors alike to engage in a maritime celebration that pays homage to the city's coastal heritage. The open-air theaters and lively street performances further solidify Le Havre as a stage where cultures collide and stories are shared in myriad ways.

Venturing beyond the city's confines unveils a world of outdoor pursuits and adventures. From exploring serene parks and gardens to engaging in exhilarating water sports, Le Havre caters to those seeking both tranquility and excitement. And for the intrepid traveler, nearby destinations like the iconic cliffs of Étretat offer breathtaking vistas that showcase nature's artistry on a grand scale.

Le Havre's significance resonates not only within its boundaries but also within the broader context of Normandy's landscape. The city's role as a gateway to the region allows travelers to embark on journeys of exploration to neighboring towns, villages, and natural wonders. This connectivity showcases the symbiotic relationship between Le Havre and its surroundings, enriching the tapestry of experiences available to all who journey there.

CHAPTER 1: Planning Your Trip

When to Visit: Best Seasons and Events

Le Havre's beauty shines year-round, each season offering a unique charm and a calendar brimming with events that enhance your experience. Here's a guide to the best seasons to visit and the noteworthy events that grace this coastal city:

Spring (March - May)

Spring in Le Havre heralds the awakening of nature and the city's cultural scene. As flowers bloom and temperatures rise, it's an ideal time to explore the city's parks, gardens, and outdoor spaces. The Jardins Suspendus, or Hanging Gardens, come alive with vibrant colors and panoramic views of the city. In April, the Printemps du Livre literary festival invites authors and readers to celebrate literature through discussions, workshops, and book fairs.

Summer (June - August)

Summer is the peak tourist season in Le Havre, and for good reason. The warm and pleasant weather makes it perfect for enjoying the city's beaches and seaside promenades. The Fête de la Musique on June 21st brings music to the streets, and July welcomes the annual Festival de la Mer, a maritime celebration featuring regattas, boat races, and cultural events. This is also a great time for outdoor markets and exploring the Normandy countryside.

Fall (September - November)

Autumn paints Le Havre with a golden hue, and the city's cultural offerings continue to thrive. September marks the Journées du Patrimoine (Heritage Days), when historic sites open their doors to the public, offering a glimpse into the city's rich history. The Musique à Beauregard festival brings classical music to unique venues across Le Havre. Fall is also a perfect time for food enthusiasts to savor local harvests and culinary events.

Winter (December - February)

While temperatures dip, Le Havre's warmth extends to its festive ambiance during the winter months. The city is adorned with holiday lights and decorations, creating a cozy atmosphere. December brings Christmas markets, ice skating rinks, and seasonal concerts that invite visitors to embrace the holiday spirit. January sees the arrival of the Fête de la Galette, a celebration of the traditional galette des rois pastry.

Year-Round Cultural Attractions

No matter when you visit, Le Havre's cultural attractions are open year-round. Museums like MuMa (Musée d'Art Moderne André Malraux) showcase art spanning centuries, while the Maison de l'Armateur offers insights into the city's maritime history. The Maison de l'Étudiant Cultural Center hosts performances and events, providing a glimpse into the city's creative heart.

Le Havre's best season to visit depends on your preferences. Spring and fall offer mild weather and cultural events, while summer brings the excitement of festivals and beachside activities.

Winter transforms the city into a holiday wonderland. Whatever the season, Le Havre welcomes you with open arms, promising an unforgettable experience steeped in both natural beauty and cultural richness.

Packing List for your adventure

Clothing and Accessories

Comfortable walking shoes for exploring cities, towns, and natural sites.

Light rain jacket or waterproof shell for unpredictable weather.

Sweaters or layers for cooler evenings and changing temperatures.

Swimsuit if you plan to enjoy the beaches or go swimming.

Sun hat, sunglasses, and sunscreen to protect against sun exposure.

Casual and semi-formal outfits for dining at restaurants.

Scarf or shawl for versatility and warmth.

Sleepwear and undergarments.

Hat, gloves, and a warm coat if traveling during colder months.

Electronics

Smartphone, charger, and portable power bank for staying connected.

Camera or smartphone with a good camera for capturing memories.

Adapters and converters for charging your electronics.

Travel Essentials

Valid passport and any required visas.

Printed copies of travel documents, including hotel reservations and itineraries.

Travel insurance documents and emergency contact information.

Wallet with credit/debit cards, cash, and identification.

Reusable water bottle to stay hydrated on the go.

Small daypack for carrying essentials during outings.

First aid kit with basic medications, bandages, and any personal prescriptions.

Toiletries
Toothbrush, toothpaste, and other personal hygiene items.

Shampoo, conditioner, and soap (consider eco-friendly options).

Skincare products, including moisturizer and lip balm.

Hairbrush or comb.

Feminine hygiene products if needed.

Miscellaneous
Travel guidebook or maps of the region.

Language phrasebook or translation app to help with communication.

Local currency for small purchases and tips.

Snacks and reusable utensils for picnics and on-the-go meals.

Entertainment options like books, magazines, or puzzles for downtime.

Specific Items for Coastal Adventures
Beach towel or mat for beach outings.

Sandals or flip-flops for beach and water activities.

Beach bag to carry essentials like sunscreen, water, and snacks.

Health and Safety

Prescription medications and necessary medical supplies.

Insect repellent for outdoor activities.

Basic first aid items such as adhesive bandages and antiseptic wipes.

Remember that the key to packing is to strike a balance between essentials and avoiding overpacking. Pack items that serve multiple purposes and prioritize comfort and practicality.

Practical Information: Travel Essentials and Local Tips

1. Accommodation
Le Havre offers a range of accommodation options, including hotels, bed and breakfasts, and vacation rentals.

Book accommodations in advance, especially during peak tourist seasons, to secure your preferred stay.

2. Transportation
Le Havre is well-connected by train, with regular services to and from major cities like Paris and Rouen.

Local buses provide convenient transportation within the city, and taxis are readily available.

3. Currency and Payment
The currency used in France is the Euro (EUR). Credit and debit cards are widely accepted, but it's advisable to have some cash on hand for small purchases or in case you encounter places that don't accept cards.

4. Language
French is the official language. While many locals understand basic English, learning a few common French phrases can be helpful and appreciated.

5. Weather and Clothing
The weather can vary depending on the season. Pack accordingly with layers, comfortable walking shoes, and weather-appropriate clothing.

Don't forget to bring a light jacket or sweater, even in summer, as coastal areas can get breezy.

6. Health and Safety

Le Havre is generally safe for tourists. However, always be cautious of your belongings, especially in crowded areas.

European health insurance cards (EHIC) or travel insurance are recommended to cover any medical emergencies.

7. Local Etiquette

When dining in restaurants, it's customary to greet the staff with a polite "Bonjour" before placing your order.

Tipping is not obligatory, as service charges are often included, but leaving a small tip for exceptional service is appreciated.

8. Opening Hours

Shops and businesses typically follow regular hours, closing for a break during lunchtime (around 12:00 PM to 2:00 PM).

Many smaller shops and businesses may close on Sundays, so plan your shopping accordingly.

9. Tourist Information

Le Havre has a tourist office where you can get maps, brochures, and information about events and attractions.

Tourist offices often provide guided tours that offer insights into the city's history and culture.

10. Internet and Connectivity

Le Havre has good mobile network coverage and public Wi-Fi is available in many cafes, restaurants, and public areas.

Consider getting a local SIM card for internet access if needed during your stay.

11. Cultural Sensitivity

Respect local customs and traditions, and dress modestly when visiting religious sites.

Keep noise levels down, especially in residential areas, during the evenings.

12. **Environment and Sustainability**
France is committed to environmental sustainability. Look for recycling bins and eco-friendly practices during your stay.

By keeping these practical tips in mind, you'll be well-equipped to navigate Le Havre with ease and make the most of your journey, whether you're exploring its cultural attractions, embracing its maritime charm, or indulging in its culinary delights.

Transportation Options: Getting to and Around Le Havre

Navigating transportation to and within Le Havre is an essential aspect of your trip planning. Here's a detailed guide to transportation options that will help you get to and around this coastal city with ease:

Getting to Le Havre
By Train: Le Havre is well-connected by train to major French cities. The city's train station, Gare du Havre, receives regular services from

destinations like Paris, Rouen, and Caen. High-speed trains (TGV) offer efficient travel options.

By Car: If you prefer driving, highways link Le Havre to other regions in France. The A29 and A131 highways provide convenient access by road. Parking is available throughout the city, but it's recommended to check parking options near your accommodation in advance.

By Air: The nearest major airport to Le Havre is the Deauville-Normandie Airport (DOL), located about an hour's drive away. From the airport, you can take a taxi or rent a car to reach Le Havre.

Getting Around Le Havre
Public Transportation: Le Havre's public transportation system includes buses that connect various parts of the city. The Bus Océane network covers a wide area and is a cost-effective way to explore. You can purchase tickets onboard or at designated ticket outlets.

Biking: Le Havre is a bike-friendly city with dedicated bike lanes and rental services.

Renting a bike is an eco-friendly and enjoyable way to explore the city's streets, promenades, and parks.

Walking: Many of Le Havre's attractions are within walking distance of each other. Strolling through the city allows you to soak in its unique architecture, coastal views, and local ambiance.

Taxis and Ridesharing: Taxis are readily available in Le Havre and can be hailed on the street or booked in advance. Ridesharing services like Uber may also operate in the city.

Useful Tips

City Transportation Pass: Consider purchasing a multi-day transportation pass for unlimited bus rides within the city. These passes are convenient and can save you money if you plan to use public transportation frequently.

Renting a Car: While public transportation is efficient, if you plan to explore the surrounding Normandy region extensively, renting a car might be a convenient option.

Traffic and Parking: If you're driving, be aware of traffic regulations and parking rules. Some areas in the city center may have limited parking, so it's advisable to use designated parking lots.

Bike Rentals: Le Havre's bike rental services often include helmets and locks. Familiarize yourself with bike lanes and follow traffic rules while cycling.

Walking Tours: Consider joining guided walking tours to discover the city's hidden gems and learn about its history and culture from local guides.

By understanding the transportation options available, you can seamlessly plan your journey to Le Havre and make the most of your time exploring the city and its surroundings. Whether you're arriving by train, car, or air, and whether you choose to bike, walk, or use public transportation, Le Havre's charms await your discovery.

CHAPTER 2: Unveiling Le Havre's Essence

The History of Le Havre: From Past to Present

The history of Le Havre is a tale of resilience, transformation, and cultural evolution. From its humble beginnings as a small fishing village to its status as a modern UNESCO World Heritage Site, Le Havre's journey through time is a testament to the enduring spirit of its people and the power of innovation.

Early Settlements
Le Havre's history dates back centuries to a time when it was a small coastal settlement known for fishing and trading. The village's strategic location along the English Channel contributed to its growth as a maritime hub, connecting Normandy to other regions.

Birth of Le Havre
In 1517, King Francis I of France recognized the potential of the natural harbor and ordered

the construction of a fortified port. The city's name, "Le Havre," translates to "the harbor" in English, reflecting its newfound purpose. The harbor's development led to increased trade and the emergence of Le Havre as a significant port city.

Economic Growth and Challenges
Le Havre continued to thrive as a major port during the 17th and 18th centuries. The city's prosperity was driven by its maritime activities, trade routes, and shipbuilding industry. However, Le Havre also faced challenges, including periods of war and economic downturns that affected its growth.

World War II and Reconstruction
One of the most significant chapters in Le Havre's history occurred during World War II. The city suffered extensive damage from bombings, and its port facilities were heavily targeted. After the war, the reconstruction efforts led by architect Auguste Perret transformed Le Havre's landscape. Perret's innovative use of reinforced concrete resulted in a new city center characterized by modernist architecture.

Modern Era and UNESCO Recognition
The post-war reconstruction marked a turning point in Le Havre's history. In 2005, the city's rebuilt center, showcasing a unique blend of historical and modern architecture, was designated a UNESCO World Heritage Site. This recognition highlighted the city's role as a living testament to urban planning and architectural innovation.

Cultural and Artistic Heritage
Le Havre's cultural significance extends beyond its architecture. The city has been an inspiration for artists, including the renowned painter Claude Monet. His "Impression, Sunrise" painting, which is credited with giving the Impressionist movement its name, depicts the harbor of Le Havre.

Contemporary Le Havre
Today, Le Havre stands as a vibrant and forward-looking city, embracing its maritime heritage while fostering cultural diversity and artistic expression. The city's museums, festivals, and cultural events celebrate its history and contribute to its dynamic atmosphere.

From its humble beginnings as a fishing village to its modern-day status as a hub of art, culture, and innovation, Le Havre's history is a tapestry woven with the threads of time. Its journey from past to present is a reminder that cities can evolve, adapt, and flourish in the face of challenges, leaving a legacy that inspires generations to come.

Architectural Marvels: Exploring the City's Unique Structures

Le Havre's architectural marvels stand as a testament to the city's resilience, creativity, and innovative spirit. From the harmonious blend of historical and modern structures to the unique designs that define its cityscape, Le Havre's architecture is a treasure trove waiting to be explored.

1. **Perret's Reconstruction**
The reconstruction of Le Havre after World War II was led by architect Auguste Perret. His pioneering use of reinforced concrete resulted in

buildings that combined functionality with aesthetic appeal.

Perret's most iconic creation is the Volcan, a cultural center that houses a theater and a library. Its cubic design and the use of glass and concrete create a dynamic visual impact.

2. **Le Havre Cathedral**
The Cathédrale Notre-Dame du Havre is a remarkable blend of the old and the new. While the original cathedral was largely destroyed during the war, its reconstructed facade preserves the historical essence, while the interior features modern design elements.

3. **Maison de l'Armateur**
This 18th-century mansion is a testament to Le Havre's maritime heritage. It showcases the opulence of ship owners from the past and offers insights into the city's historical connections to the sea.

4. **Oscar Niemeyer's Le Volcan**
Designed by the renowned Brazilian architect Oscar Niemeyer, Le Volcan is a striking example of modernist architecture. Its

curvilinear form and use of concrete create a sense of fluidity and movement, paying homage to Le Havre's maritime identity.

5. Eglise Saint-Joseph

The Église Saint-Joseph is a towering masterpiece of contemporary architecture. Its 107-meter spire dominates the skyline and serves as a beacon visible from both land and sea. The church's unique design was inspired by the shape of an ocean liner.

6. Les Bains des Docks

Designed by Jean Nouvel, Les Bains des Docks is a modern aquatic center characterized by its bold colors and geometric forms. The interplay of light and space within the building creates a captivating visual experience.

7. Musée d'Art Moderne André Malraux (MuMa)

The MuMa is not only a cultural treasure but also an architectural gem. Its expansive glass facade allows natural light to illuminate the impressive collection of Impressionist and modern art within.

8. University of Le Havre

The University of Le Havre's campus features a mix of contemporary and eco-friendly structures. The modern design fosters a conducive learning environment while embracing sustainability principles.

9. Les Docks Vauban

This former warehouse complex has been repurposed into a vibrant commercial and cultural space. The juxtaposition of old industrial elements with modern renovations offers a captivating atmosphere for shopping, dining, and entertainment.

10. Maison de l'Étudiant

Designed by Jacques Tournant, this cultural center is a masterpiece of modern architecture. Its fluid lines and innovative use of materials create a space that is both functional and visually striking.

Exploring Le Havre's architectural marvels is like embarking on a journey through time and design innovation. Each structure tells a story, whether it's the resilience of the post-war reconstruction or the creative expression of contemporary architects. As you wander through the city's streets, you'll find that Le Havre's architectural treasures are not just buildings; they are a living testament to human ingenuity and the city's enduring spirit.

Art and Culture: Museums, Galleries, and Cultural Highlights

1. **Musée d'Art Moderne André Malraux (MuMa)**

Location: 2 Boulevard Clemenceau, 76600 Le Havre

MuMa is a treasure trove of Impressionist and modern art, boasting works by Monet, Renoir, Degas, and more. Its stunning glass facade and extensive collection make it a cultural icon.

The museum's collection spans various artistic movements, offering insights into the evolution of art over the centuries.

2. Maison de l'Armateur

Location: 3 Quai de l'Ile, 76600 Le Havre

This 18th-century mansion is a testament to Le Havre's maritime heritage. It showcases opulent interiors and offers a glimpse into the lives of ship owners of yesteryears.

The museum provides an immersive experience of the city's history and connections to the sea.

3. Maison de l'Étudiant

Location: 50 Rue Jean-Jacques Rousseau, 76600 Le Havre

This modern cultural center is a hub for artistic expression. It hosts exhibitions, performances, workshops, and events that celebrate a diverse range of creative endeavors.

From visual arts to music and theater, the Maison de l'Étudiant fosters a lively atmosphere of artistic exchange.

4. Le Tetris

Location: 33 Rue du 329e, 76620 Le Havre

Le Tetris is a dynamic cultural space that hosts concerts, exhibitions, and events that span various genres and disciplines.

This venue is known for its energetic ambiance and its dedication to promoting emerging artists and alternative forms of expression.

5. Le Volcan - Scène Nationale du Havre
Location: 8 Place de l'Hôtel de Ville, 76600 Le Havre

Le Volcan is not only an architectural marvel but also a hub for performing arts. The theater hosts plays, dance performances, concerts, and other cultural events.

Its programming reflects the city's commitment to artistic diversity and innovation.

6. Ateliers 30
Location: 30 Rue Jules Lecesne, 76600 Le Havre

Ateliers 30 is an art space that offers a platform for local artists to create, exhibit, and engage with the community.

It's a space where visitors can witness the creative process and explore contemporary art from the region.

7. **Art Galleries**
Le Havre boasts a range of art galleries that feature works by local and international artists.

Galleries like Galerie Hamon and Galerie Dufay-Bonnet showcase diverse artistic styles and mediums.

8. **Street Art and Murals**
Le Havre's streets are an open-air gallery, adorned with vibrant murals and street art installations. The city's commitment to public art adds an extra layer of cultural richness to its urban landscape.

9. **Cultural Events**
Le Havre hosts a variety of cultural events, from film festivals to music concerts. Keep an eye on the city's event calendar to catch exhibitions, performances, and festivals that showcase its artistic dynamism.

10. Le Havre Biennale

The Le Havre Biennale is a major cultural event that takes place every two years. It showcases contemporary art from both local and international artists, creating a dynamic platform for artistic dialogue and exploration.

The biennale features exhibitions, installations, performances, and talks that engage with pressing social, cultural, and artistic themes.

11. Cultural Festivals

Le Havre's festivals celebrate a range of artistic disciplines. The Fête de la Musique brings music to the streets, while the Festival de la Mer celebrates the city's maritime heritage through regattas, boat races, and cultural events.

12. Jean-François Millet's Birthplace

Location: 46 Grande Rue, 76620 Greville-Hague

Although not located within Le Havre itself, the nearby birthplace of artist Jean-François Millet is of historical and artistic significance. Millet's iconic painting "The Gleaners" is celebrated worldwide.

13. **Normandy Impressionist Festival**
Le Havre often participates in the Normandy Impressionist Festival, a regional celebration of Impressionist art and culture. This festival offers exhibitions, performances, and events across Normandy.

14. **Public Art Installations**
Le Havre's commitment to public art extends beyond traditional galleries. The city often hosts temporary art installations in public spaces, encouraging residents and visitors to engage with art in unexpected places.

15. **Art and Craft Markets**
Explore Le Havre's markets to discover local artisans and their creations. These markets offer a range of handmade crafts, paintings, jewelry, and other unique items that reflect the city's artistic spirit.

From its world-class museums to its grassroots art spaces, Le Havre's art and culture scene offers a rich and immersive experience.

CHAPTER 3: Coastal Charm and Scenic Splendor

The Seaside Beauty: Beaches and Seascapes

Le Havre's coastline is a haven of seaside beauty, offering stunning beaches and seascapes that invite relaxation, recreation, and exploration.

1. **Plage du Havre (Le Havre Beach)**
Location: Along the coast of Le Havre

Le Havre Beach is the city's primary beach, featuring a long stretch of golden sand. It's perfect for sunbathing, picnicking, and leisurely walks along the water's edge.

The beach offers breathtaking views of the sea and the city's modernist architecture, creating a unique juxtaposition of nature and urban design.

2. Plage de Sainte-Adresse

Location: Rue du Docteur Lemaire, 76310 Sainte-Adresse (adjacent to Le Havre)

This tranquil beach is located in the neighboring town of Sainte-Adresse, just a short distance from Le Havre. It offers a quieter atmosphere and picturesque surroundings.

The beach is known for its panoramic views of the sea and the iconic cliffs of Étretat in the distance.

3. Plage de Saint-Jouin-Bruneval

Location: Rue de la Plage, 76280 Saint-Jouin-Bruneval (near Le Havre)

This charming pebble beach is situated in the village of Saint-Jouin-Bruneval, a short drive from Le Havre. It's known for its serene ambiance and stunning vistas.

The beach is ideal for quiet contemplation, beachcombing, and enjoying the calming sounds of the waves.

4. Plage du Butin

Location: Rue du Butin, 76620 Le Havre

Plage du Butin is a small and cozy beach that offers a more secluded setting. Its sheltered cove provides a peaceful environment for relaxation.

The beach is popular among locals seeking a tranquil escape, and it's an excellent spot to watch the sun set over the horizon.

5. Seascapes and Coastal Views

Le Havre's coastline is adorned with picturesque seascapes and stunning viewpoints. The cliffs of Étretat, located a short drive away, are an iconic natural wonder that should not be missed.

Walk along the promenades and piers to enjoy panoramic vistas of the sea, watch fishing boats sail by, and immerse yourself in the maritime ambiance.

6. **Water Activities**
Le Havre's beaches offer opportunities for water sports such as swimming, kiteboarding, and paddleboarding. The gentle waves and clear waters make it a safe and enjoyable environment for aquatic adventures.

7. **Beachfront Cafes and Restaurants**
Along the coast, you'll find a variety of cafes and restaurants that offer seaside dining experiences. Enjoy fresh seafood, local specialties, and stunning ocean views.

Le Havre's beaches and seascapes are a treasure trove of natural beauty and tranquility.

Strolling Along the Promenade: Beachfront Activities

Strolling along Le Havre's promenades offers a delightful blend of beachfront activities, scenic views, and a refreshing ocean breeze. Here's a guide to the charming beachfront activities you can enjoy while leisurely strolling along the city's picturesque promenades:

1. **Relaxing on the Beach**
Find a cozy spot on the sandy shores to relax, read a book, or simply soak up the sun. The gentle sounds of the waves create a serene backdrop for unwinding.

2. **Beach Picnics**
Pack a picnic basket with your favorite snacks and enjoy a leisurely meal with a view. The beachfront provides a perfect setting for a delightful picnic with friends or family.

3. **People-Watching**
As you stroll along the promenade, take a moment to people-watch. Observe locals and tourists engaging in various activities, creating a vibrant and lively atmosphere.

4. **Artistic Inspiration**
The stunning coastal vistas and play of light on the water make for perfect artistic inspiration. Bring along a sketchbook or a camera to capture the beauty of the surroundings.

5. **Seaside Photography**
Capture memories of your time in Le Havre by taking photographs of the picturesque landscapes, the city's unique architecture, and the sea.

6. **Beach Games**
Pack a beach ball, frisbee, or paddleboard for some beachside fun. Engage in friendly games and activities with friends and family as you enjoy the ocean breeze.

7. **Coastal Cafes and Refreshments**
Along the promenade, you'll find cafes and stalls offering refreshments. Take a break to enjoy a cup of coffee, an ice cream cone, or a cool drink while gazing at the sea.

8. **Cycling and Rollerblading**
Many promenades are pedestrian-friendly and offer designated paths for cycling and rollerblading. Rent a bike or bring your own to enjoy a scenic ride by the sea.

9. **Sunset Views**

The promenade is an ideal location to catch breathtaking sunsets over the horizon. Watch as the sky transforms into a palette of vibrant colors, casting a warm glow over the sea.

10. **Romantic Strolls**

The tranquil ambiance of the promenade makes it a perfect spot for a romantic stroll with a loved one. The sound of the waves and the beauty of the sea provide a romantic backdrop.

11. **Seafood Delights**

Explore the nearby seafood restaurants and enjoy a meal by the sea. Indulge in fresh catches of the day and savor the flavors of Normandy's coastal cuisine.

Strolling along Le Havre's promenades is a sensory experience that invites you to engage with the beauty of the sea, the energy of the city, and the relaxation of a leisurely walk.

Day Trips to Nearby Coastal Wonders

Le Havre's strategic location along the Normandy coast makes it an excellent starting point for day trips to nearby coastal wonders. Here are some coastal destinations you can explore, along with information on how to get there from Le Havre:

1. **Étretat**

Location: Approximately 35 km northwest of Le Havre

Known for its iconic chalk cliffs and natural arches, Étretat is a must-visit destination for its breathtaking coastal landscapes.

How to Get There: Take a train from Le Havre to Étretat (via Bréauté-Beuzeville). Alternatively, you can drive or take a guided tour.

2. **Honfleur**

Location: Approximately 25 km east of Le Havre

Honfleur is a charming harbor town famous for its picturesque Old Port, historic buildings, and maritime heritage.

How to Get There: Drive to Honfleur in about 30 minutes or take a bus from Le Havre to Honfleur. Guided tours are also available.

3. Deauville and Trouville-sur-Mer
Location: Approximately 50 km southeast of Le Havre

Deauville and Trouville-sur-Mer are known for their upscale resorts, sandy beaches, and lively atmosphere.

How to Get There: Take a train from Le Havre to Trouville-Deauville station. The journey takes around 1 hour. Driving is also an option.

4. Fécamp
Location: Approximately 35 km northeast of Le Havre

Fécamp is a historic port town with attractions such as the stunning Benedictine Palace and the Abbaye de la Trinité.

How to Get There: Take a train from Le Havre to Fécamp (via Bréauté-Beuzeville). The journey takes around 1 hour.

5. Veules-les-Roses

Location: Approximately 85 km east of Le Havre

Veules-les-Roses is a charming village known for having the shortest river in France, charming cottages, and a peaceful ambiance.

How to Get There: Drive to Veules-les-Roses in about 1.5 hours or take a train from Le Havre to Yvetot and then a taxi or bus to Veules-les-Roses.

6. Le Tilleul and Vaucottes

Location: Along the coast between Le Havre and Étretat

These lesser-known villages offer serene beaches, cliffs, and beautiful coastal walks.

How to Get There: Drive along the coastal road (D940) from Le Havre to Étretat, stopping at these villages along the way.

7. Dieppe

Location: Approximately 105 km east of Le Havre

Dieppe is a historic port town with a charming harbor, pebble beaches, and a castle overlooking the sea.

How to Get There: Drive to Dieppe in about 1.5 hours or take a train from Le Havre to Dieppe.

Whether you're seeking dramatic cliffs, charming villages, or lively coastal towns, Le Havre's proximity to these coastal wonders allows for a variety of day trip options. Consider your interests, travel preferences, and available transportation when planning your coastal explorations from Le Havre.

CHAPTER 4: Culinary Delights and Gastronomic Adventures

A Taste of Normandy: Local Cuisine and Specialties

Indulging in Normandy's local cuisine and specialties is a culinary journey that captures the essence of the region's rich flavors and traditions. Here's a delectable guide to some of Normandy's most iconic dishes and where to savor them:

1. **Camembert Cheese**
Normandy is renowned for its creamy and aromatic Camembert cheese. This soft cheese is often enjoyed with fresh bread, paired with fruits, or melted into dishes.

Where to Try: Local markets, cheese shops, and restaurants throughout Normandy.

2. **Normandy Apple Cider**
The region's apple orchards produce high-quality apples that are transformed into refreshing apple ciders. Normandy's ciders come in various styles, from sweet to dry.

Where to Try: Visit cider farms, local markets, and traditional pubs for a taste of authentic Normandy cider.

3. **Seafood Platters**
Normandy's coastal location ensures an abundance of fresh seafood. Seafood platters often include oysters, mussels, clams, shrimp, and other delicacies.

Where to Try: Coastal restaurants and seafood markets, particularly in towns like Le Havre and Honfleur.

4. **Galettes and Crêpes**
Normandy is famous for its savory galettes (buckwheat pancakes) and sweet crêpes. Galettes are typically filled with ingredients like cheese, ham, and eggs, while crêpes are adorned with sweet fillings.

Where to Try: Crêperies and restaurants serving traditional Breton cuisine.

5. Norman Cream

La crème normande, or Norman cream, is a rich and luxurious dessert made with cream, eggs, and sugar. It's often flavored with vanilla or a splash of Calvados (apple brandy).

Where to Try: Dessert shops, patisseries, and traditional Norman restaurants.

6. Andouille Sausage

Andouille sausage is a smoky and flavorful delicacy made from pork intestines and tripe. It's often used in soups, stews, and traditional Norman dishes.

Where to Try: Butcher shops, charcuteries, and local markets.

7. Coquilles Saint-Jacques (Scallops)

Normandy's scallops are a culinary highlight. Coquilles Saint-Jacques are often pan-seared and served with a creamy sauce, creating a delectable seafood dish.

Where to Try: Seafood restaurants and gourmet eateries.

8. Tarte Tatin

This beloved dessert features caramelized apples baked under a flaky pastry crust. Tarte Tatin is typically served warm and pairs perfectly with a scoop of vanilla ice cream.

Where to Try: Patisseries, bakeries, and dessert cafes.

9. Calvados

Calvados is a renowned apple brandy produced in Normandy. It's often enjoyed as an aperitif or after a meal as a digestif.

Where to Try: Distilleries, specialty liquor stores, and restaurants.

10. Normandy Cream Pies

Normandy's cream pies, such as teurgoule (rice pudding) and flaugnarde (fruit-filled dessert), are beloved comfort foods with a touch of sweetness.

Where to Try: Traditional Normandy restaurants and bakeries.

Exploring Normandy's local cuisine is a delightful way to immerse yourself in the region's culture and culinary heritage. Whether you're savoring creamy cheeses, sipping apple cider, or indulging in seafood delights, each bite offers a taste of Normandy's unique and delicious identity.

Dining Options: Restaurants, Cafes, and Food Markets

1. **Restaurants**

Le Havre boasts a variety of restaurants that serve both traditional Norman cuisine and international dishes. From seafood delights to hearty stews, you'll find a range of options to satisfy your palate.

Recommended Restaurants in Le Havre
Restaurant Le Grignot (7 Place de l'Hôtel de Ville, 76600 Le Havre): A cozy bistro offering French classics and seafood dishes.

Le Chalut (52 Quai de Southampton, 76600 Le Havre): A seafood restaurant with picturesque views of the harbor.

Au Cœur du Moka (22 Rue de Paris, 76600 Le Havre): Known for its inventive cuisine and elegant ambiance.

2. **Cafes and Bakeries**
Enjoying a leisurely coffee or tea in a cozy cafe is a quintessential experience. Normandy's cafes often feature freshly baked pastries and treats.

Recommended Cafes in Le Havre
Café du Musée (2 Boulevard Clemenceau, 76600 Le Havre): Located near MuMa, it offers a charming setting to enjoy coffee and desserts.
Salon de Thé Charlotte Corday (16 Rue Louis Brindeau, 76600 Le Havre): A tea salon with a wide selection of teas and pastries.

3. **Seafood Shacks and Huts**
Along the coast, you'll find seafood shacks and huts serving freshly caught seafood. These casual spots offer a taste of the sea in a relaxed atmosphere.

Locations: Look for these shacks along the harbors of Le Havre and nearby coastal towns.

4. Food Markets

Normandy's food markets are a treasure trove of fresh produce, cheeses, meats, and other local specialties. Strolling through these markets is a sensory experience.

Recommended Food Markets in Le Havre

Les Halles Centrales (Place de l'Hôtel de Ville, 76600 Le Havre): A covered market offering a wide variety of products, from fruits and vegetables to cheeses and meats.

Marché de l'Hôtel de Ville (Place de l'Hôtel de Ville, 76600 Le Havre): A weekly market where you can find local and regional products.

5. Gourmet Experiences

If you're seeking gourmet dining experiences, consider exploring Michelin-starred restaurants that showcase the finest of Norman cuisine.

Notable Michelin-starred Restaurants in Normandy:

Sa.Qua.Na (22 Place Hamelin, 14600 Honfleur): A renowned restaurant offering creative cuisine that celebrates local ingredients. Auberge du Vieux Puits (5 Rue de l'Église, 50240 Valognes): A gourmet restaurant known for its refined dishes and elegant setting.

6. **Local Specialties**
Don't miss the opportunity to savor Normandy's specialties, including Camembert cheese, apple cider, and seafood platters. These can be enjoyed in various dining establishments across the region.

Wine and Dine: Pairing Your Meals with Local Wines

Pairing your meals with local wines is a delightful way to enhance your culinary experience in Normandy. The region offers a range of wines that complement its diverse cuisine.

1. **Seafood and White Wines**
Normandy's coastal location makes seafood a prominent part of its cuisine. Fresh seafood dishes, such as oysters, mussels, and fish, pair wonderfully with crisp and refreshing white wines.

Recommended White Wines
Muscadet: This light and citrusy wine enhances the flavors of delicate seafood.

Chardonnay: A well-balanced Chardonnay can complement a variety of seafood dishes with its acidity and fruitiness.

2. **Cheese and Cider**
Normandy is known for its creamy cheeses, and cider is a popular local beverage. The acidity of cider can cut through the richness of cheeses, creating a harmonious pairing.

Recommended Ciders
Normandy Apple Cider: The region's signature drink, with its apple notes and varying levels of sweetness, pairs well with a variety of cheeses.

3. Duck and Red Wines

For heartier dishes like duck confit or roasted meats, consider pairing with red wines. The robust flavors of red wines complement the savory notes of these dishes.

Recommended Red Wines
Pinot Noir: A light and elegant red wine that works well with roasted meats and game dishes.

Cabernet Franc: This red wine offers earthy and herbaceous notes that can complement the flavors of duck.

4. Tarte Tatin and Dessert Wines

Normandy's famous Tarte Tatin, a caramelized apple dessert, pairs beautifully with dessert wines that have a touch of sweetness.

Recommended Dessert Wines
Apple-Based Aperitifs: Normandy offers apple-based liqueurs that can be served as aperitifs or paired with desserts like Tarte Tatin.

5. Camembert and Rosé Wine
The rich and creamy Camembert cheese can be balanced with a light and fruity rosé wine.

Recommended Rosé Wines
Local Rosé: Look for rosé wines produced in the region, which often offer fruity and floral notes that complement the cheese.

6. Calvados and Digestifs
After your meal, consider enjoying a glass of Calvados, Normandy's renowned apple brandy, as a digestive.

Recommended Digestifs
Calvados: A traditional choice that encapsulates the flavors of the region.

When pairing wine with your meals in Normandy, keep in mind that the goal is to create a harmonious balance of flavors. Consider the flavors and textures of both the dish and the wine to ensure a delightful dining experience.

CHAPTER 5: Elegance and Entertainment

Shopping in Style: Boutiques, Souvenirs, and Local Crafts

1. **Boutiques and Shops**
Le Havre and other towns in Normandy are home to charming boutiques that offer fashion, home decor, and other distinctive items.

Recommended Shopping Areas in Le Havre
Rue de Paris: This bustling street in the city center features a mix of fashion boutiques, gift shops, and more.

Les Docks Vauban: A modern shopping complex with a variety of stores, cafes, and restaurants.

2. **Local Souvenirs**
When shopping for souvenirs, consider items that reflect the culture and traditions of Normandy.

Recommended Souvenirs

Camembert Cheese: Bring back a wheel of this iconic cheese, either to enjoy during your trip or as a gift.

Apple-Based Products: Look for apple ciders, jams, and other treats made from the region's apples.

Calvados: A bottle of Normandy's famous apple brandy makes for a memorable and authentic souvenir.

Linens and Textiles: Normandy is known for its quality linens and fabrics, so consider items like tablecloths and tea towels.

3. **Traditional Crafts**
Normandy is rich in traditional crafts that make for unique and meaningful souvenirs.

Recommended Crafts

Pottery and Ceramics: Look for handmade pottery, plates, and bowls crafted by local artisans.

Lace and Embroidery: Normandy has a long tradition of intricate lacework and embroidery. Woodcrafts: Wooden items such as cutting boards, bowls, and decorative pieces are often available in local markets.

4. Farmers' Markets
Farmers' markets are a great place to find fresh produce, cheeses, and artisanal products.

Recommended Farmers' Markets in Le Havre

Marché de l'Hôtel de Ville (Place de l'Hôtel de Ville, 76600 Le Havre): A weekly market with a variety of local goods.

Les Halles Centrales (Place de l'Hôtel de Ville, 76600 Le Havre): A covered market offering fresh produce, cheeses, and more.

5. Antique Shops and Flea Markets
If you're a fan of antiques and vintage finds, Normandy's antique shops and flea markets are worth exploring.

Recommended Antique Shops and Flea Markets:

Le Havre Antiquités (25 Rue de Paris, 76600 Le Havre): A shop with a variety of antique and vintage items.

Brocante de Graville (Place Pierre-Bérégovoy, 76600 Le Havre): A flea market where you might discover unique treasures.

6. **Local Art Galleries**
Consider exploring local art galleries for original artworks, prints, and other artistic creations.

Look for galleries and art spaces in Le Havre and other towns, showcasing the work of regional artists.

Shopping in Normandy allows you to bring home a piece of the region's culture, craftsmanship, and flavors.

Nightlife and Entertainment: Bars, Theatres, and Evening Activities

1. **Bars and Pubs**

Normandy's towns and cities come alive after dark with a selection of bars and pubs where you can enjoy drinks, socialize, and soak up the local atmosphere.

Recommended Bars in Le Havre

La Cave à Bières (36 Rue Jules Lecesne, 76600 Le Havre): A cozy bar offering a wide selection of beers.

L'Exocet (41 Rue de Paris, 76600 Le Havre): A popular cocktail bar known for its creative drinks.

2. **Theatres and Performing Arts**

If you're interested in cultural entertainment, Normandy's theaters and performing arts venues offer a variety of shows and performances.

Recommended Theatres in Normandy

Théâtre de l'Hôtel de Ville (Place de l'Hôtel de Ville, 76600 Le Havre): A historic theater that hosts a range of performances, from plays to concerts.

Le Volcan - Scène Nationale du Havre (8 Place Niemeyer, 76600 Le Havre): A contemporary cultural center with diverse artistic events.

3. Live Music Venues

Normandy's music scene comes to life at night with live performances in a range of genres.

Look for local music venues, bars, and cafes that host live music nights, featuring both local and touring artists.

4. Casino Entertainment

For a touch of excitement, consider visiting a casino in Normandy for gaming, dining, and entertainment.

Recommended Casino

Casino Barrière Deauville (2 Rue Edmond Blanc, 14800 Deauville): A renowned casino with gaming tables, slot machines, and restaurants.

5. Nighttime Events

Keep an eye out for special nighttime events, such as night markets, outdoor concerts, and cultural festivals.

Check with local tourist information centers for a schedule of upcoming events during your visit.

6. Beachside Evening Strolls

Enjoy the tranquility of the coast with evening strolls along the beaches and promenades.

Le Havre's beachfront and coastal towns like Honfleur offer picturesque settings for romantic walks.

7. Guided Night Tours

Some cities in Normandy offer guided night tours that provide a unique perspective on the region's history and architecture.

8. **Evening Dining**
Indulge in Normandy's culinary delights by dining at restaurants that offer evening hours. Many places offer special menus and ambiance for nighttime dining.

Events and Festivals: Immersing Yourself in Local Celebrations

Immersing yourself in local events and festivals is a wonderful way to experience the vibrant culture and traditions of Normandy. Here are some of the region's most notable events and festivals that you might want to consider attending:

1. **Fête de la Musique (June 21)**
This nationwide music festival celebrates the summer solstice with live music performances in streets, parks, and public spaces across Normandy.

2. **Festival Beauregard (July)**
Held in Hérouville-Saint-Clair near Caen, this music festival features a diverse lineup of artists from various genres, making it a great opportunity to enjoy live music in a beautiful setting.

3. **Armada de Rouen (Every 5 years)**
The Armada de Rouen is a spectacular maritime event that brings together an impressive fleet of tall ships from around the world. The event includes parades, concerts, and nautical festivities along the Seine River.

4. **Festival Normandie Impressionniste (Every 5 years)**
This major cultural event celebrates the Impressionist movement, which has deep roots in Normandy. Art exhibitions, performances, and various cultural activities take place across the region.

5. **Deauville American Film Festival (September):**

Film enthusiasts can enjoy screenings of American cinema classics and new releases in the elegant town of Deauville. The festival also hosts premieres, discussions, and events.

6. La Fête de la Mer (August)

Coastal towns like Le Havre and Honfleur celebrate the Sea Festival with boat parades, seafood tastings, nautical exhibitions, and various maritime-themed events.

7. Les Médiévales de Bayeux (July)

The town of Bayeux hosts a medieval festival that transports visitors back in time. Enjoy jousting, medieval crafts, costumed parades, and traditional music and dance.

8. Les Rencontres Internationales de Cerfs-Volants (April):

Held in Dieppe, this international kite festival fills the skies with colorful and creative kites from around the world. It's a unique and visually stunning event.

9. Honfleur Normandy Outlet Village (Year-round)

If you're a shopping enthusiast, you can explore outlet shopping at this village near Honfleur, offering a wide range of designer and brand-name stores.

10. Christmas Markets (December)

Many towns in Normandy host charming Christmas markets with festive decorations, local crafts, seasonal treats, and a joyful atmosphere.

CHAPTER 6: Outdoor Pursuits and Adventure

Exploring Nature: Parks, Gardens, and Outdoor Recreation

1. **Parc des Jardins Suspendus (Hanging Gardens Park)**
Address: Rue du Président René Coty, 76600 Le Havre

Located on a hill overlooking Le Havre, this park features terraced gardens, lush greenery, and panoramic views of the city and the sea.

2. **Parc Naturel Régional des Boucles de la Seine Normande (Regional Natural Park)**
Address: Maison du Parc, 99 Rue Georges-Clemenceau, 76480 Jumièges

This regional park spans the meandering loops of the Seine River and offers diverse landscapes, from wetlands and forests to chalk cliffs and cultural heritage sites.

73

3. **Bois des Moutiers**
Address: Varengeville-sur-Mer, 76119 Sainte-Marguerite-sur-Mer

This woodland garden features a stunning collection of rare and exotic plants, as well as a historic manor house.

4. **Parc Floral de la Source (Floral Park of the Source)**
Address: Route de la Source, 14123 Cormeilles

This floral park is a haven for plant enthusiasts, showcasing a wide variety of flowers, shrubs, and trees in a beautifully landscaped setting.

5. **Jardin des Plantes de Rouen (Botanical Garden)**
Address: 7 Rue de Trianon, 76000 Rouen

This historic botanical garden features themed areas, including an alpine garden, a rose garden, and a tropical greenhouse.

6. **Les Jardins d'Étretat (Gardens of Étretat)**

Address: 2 Avenue Damilaville, 76790 Étretat
These gardens offer stunning views of the Etretat cliffs and the English Channel, with unique sculptures and lush plantings.

7. Parc de Clères
Address: 1 Rue du Parc, 76690 Clères

A zoological park set in a 30-hectare landscaped park, featuring animals, birds, and a historic château.

8. Vire Canoe-Kayak
Address: Base de Loisirs de Pont D'Ouilly, 14690 Pont-d'Ouilly

Enjoy canoeing and kayaking adventures on the Vire River, surrounded by picturesque landscapes.

9. Parc des Marais (Marsh Park)
Address: Maison du Parc, 14220 Saint-Omer

This park is part of the Regional Natural Park of the Cotentin and Bessin Marshes, offering diverse flora and fauna in wetland habitats.

10. **Suisse Normande (Swiss Normandy)**
Suisse Normande is known for its hilly landscapes, gorges, and outdoor activities like hiking, rock climbing, and canoeing.

These natural spaces provide opportunities for relaxation, exploration, and outdoor activities, allowing you to experience the beauty of Normandy's diverse landscapes firsthand.

Sports and Activities: Surfing, Sailing, and More

1. **Surfing**
Normandy's coastal location makes it a great destination for surfing, particularly in towns like Étretat and Siouville-Hague.

Popular Surfing Spots: Étretat, Siouville-Hague, and Agon-Coutainville.

2. **Sailing and Boating**
With its extensive coastline and rivers, Normandy offers excellent opportunities for sailing, yachting, and boating.

Recommended Locations: Le Havre, Deauville, Honfleur, and the Seine River.

3. Hiking and Trekking

Normandy's diverse landscapes provide countless hiking and trekking trails, from coastal paths to forested hills.

Notable Trails: GR21 coastal trail, Mont-Saint-Michel Bay trail, and the Norman Bocage.

4. Horseback Riding

Explore the countryside and coastal areas on horseback through guided rides or equestrian centers.

Recommended Locations: Equestrian centers in rural areas and coastal towns.

5. Cycling

Cycling is a popular way to explore Normandy's countryside, coastal routes, and charming villages.

Cycling Routes: Avenue Verte London-Paris route, Vélo Francette route, and local cycling paths.

6. Golf

Golf enthusiasts can tee off at Normandy's scenic golf courses, some of which offer coastal views.

Notable Golf Courses: Golf Barrière Deauville, Golf d'Étretat, and Golf de Granville.

7. Rock Climbing

Adventure seekers can enjoy rock climbing on the cliffs of Normandy, particularly in the picturesque Suisse Normande region.

Recommended Areas: Suisse Normande and cliffs near Étretat.

8. Paragliding and Skydiving

Experience breathtaking views by paragliding or skydiving over Normandy's landscapes.

Recommended Locations: Paragliding centers near Clécy and skydiving centers in various towns.

9. **Fishing**
Normandy offers opportunities for both freshwater and sea fishing, with fishing charters available along the coast.

Coastal Fishing Locations: Le Havre, Honfleur, Trouville-sur-Mer, and more.

10. **Tennis and Water Sports**
Many coastal towns have facilities for tennis, beach volleyball, and water sports like jet-skiing and paddleboarding.

Thrilling Adventures: Excursions Beyond the City Limits

1. **Mont-Saint-Michel**
Explore the iconic Mont-Saint-Michel, a medieval abbey perched on a rocky island. Wander through the narrow streets, visit the abbey, and witness the mesmerizing tides.

2. **Étretat and Alabaster Coast**
Visit Étretat to witness the stunning cliffs, natural arches, and panoramic views of the

English Channel. Hike along the coastal trails for an unforgettable experience.

3. **D-Day Landing Beaches**
Discover the historic D-Day landing beaches such as Omaha Beach and Utah Beach. Museums, memorials, and bunkers provide insight into the events of World War II.

4. **Suisse Normande**
Explore the picturesque landscapes of Suisse Normande, characterized by hilly terrain, gorges, and outdoor activities like rock climbing, kayaking, and hiking.

5. **Honfleur and Seine Estuary**
Wander through the charming town of Honfleur, known for its historic harbor, cobbled streets, and art galleries. Take a boat tour to explore the Seine Estuary.

6. **Bayeux and Tapestry**
Visit Bayeux to see the famous Bayeux Tapestry, depicting the story of the Norman Conquest. The town's medieval architecture adds to its allure.

7. **Cotentin Peninsula**

Explore the Cotentin Peninsula with its rugged coastline, charming fishing villages, and the iconic La Hague headland.

8. **Rouen and Medieval Charm**
Step back in time in Rouen, known for its medieval architecture, Gothic cathedral, and connections to Joan of Arc.

9. **Cliffs and Valleys of Normandy**
Embark on a road trip through the countryside, passing by picturesque valleys, farmlands, and charming villages.

10. **Granville and Chausey Islands**
Discover the maritime town of Granville and take a boat to the Chausey Islands for a day of exploring unspoiled nature and clear waters.

CHAPTER 7: Practicalities for a Smooth Journey

Accommodation Options: Hotels, B&Bs, and Rentals

Normandy offers a wide range of accommodation options to suit various preferences and budgets. Here are some types of accommodations, along with examples and addresses:

Hotels

Le Manoir des Impressionnistes
Address: 23 Rue Saint-Siméon, 14600 Honfleur

A charming hotel set in a beautiful garden, inspired by Impressionist art and located near the heart of Honfleur.

La Ferme Saint Simeon Spa - Relais & Chateaux

Address: 20, Route Adolphe Marais, 14600 Honfleur

A luxury hotel featuring a spa and gourmet dining options, set in a historic farmhouse.

Hotel Spa Pasino

Address: Place Jules Ferry, 76600 Le Havre

A modern hotel with a spa, located near the waterfront and offering comfortable rooms.

Nomad Hotel Le Havre

Address: Rue du Maréchal Joffre, 76600 Le Havre

A contemporary hotel with stylish design, conveniently situated in the city center.

Bed and Breakfasts (B&Bs)

Le Clos de la Forge

Address: 6 Rue de la Forge, 50480 Saint-Germain-sur-Ay

A charming B&B with cozy rooms and a lovely garden, located near the coast.

Les Prés Rousselins
Address: 43 Rue aux Juifs, 14600 La Rivière-Saint-Sauveur

A welcoming B&B offering comfortable rooms and a tranquil setting close to Honfleur.

La Maison du Parc
Address: 6 rue Arsène Leloup, 76600 Le Havre

A charming B&B with comfortable rooms and a warm atmosphere, located near Parc de Rouelles.

Les Gîtes de la Mer - B&B
Address: 17 rue de l'Église, 76600 Le Havre

Cozy B&B accommodations with a maritime-inspired theme, offering a unique stay experience.

Vacation Rentals

La Maison du Pêcheur
Address: 10 Rue du Bac, 14600 Honfleur

A cozy vacation rental with a nautical theme, located in the heart of Honfleur's historic district.

La Cabane du Pêcheur
Address: Chemin des Hallettes, 76400 Senneville-sur-Fécamp

A unique seaside cabin rental offering direct access to the beach and stunning views.

Châteaux and Countryside Retreats

Château de Canisy
Address: Château de Canisy, 50750 Canisy

Experience the elegance of a historic château with luxurious rooms and serene surroundings.

Le Château de Prêtreville
Address: 49 Rue de Prêtreville, 14100 Honfleur

Stay in a charming castle near Honfleur, surrounded by lush gardens and scenic views.

Studio 1 Étoile - Le Havre

Address: Rue de la République, 76600 Le Havre

A self-contained studio apartment rental in the city center, ideal for a comfortable stay.

Le Havre Vue Mer - Apartment

Address: Avenue Foch, 76600 Le Havre

An apartment rental with sea views, perfect for enjoying the coastal atmosphere.

Campgrounds and Glamping

Camping Le Grand Large
Address: Avenue des Canadiens, 14470 Courseulles-sur-Mer

A family-friendly campground with direct access to the beach and various amenities.

Domaine de la Bucaille - Glamping
Address: La Bucaille, 14290 Saint-Cyr-du-Ronceray

Experience luxury camping in beautifully designed tents set in a tranquil estate.

Health and Safety: Tips for a Secure and Healthy Stay

Ensuring your health and safety during your stay in Normandy is crucial for a smooth and enjoyable trip. Here are some tips to help you have a secure and healthy experience:

1. **Travel Insurance**
Purchase comprehensive travel insurance that covers medical emergencies, trip cancellations, and other unexpected situations.

2. **Vaccinations and Health Precautions**
Check if any vaccinations are required before traveling. It's also a good idea to bring any necessary prescription medications and a basic first aid kit.

3. **Medical Facilities**
Familiarize yourself with the location of hospitals, clinics, and pharmacies in the area you're visiting.

4. **Hygiene Practices**
Practice good hygiene by washing your hands frequently, especially before eating. Carry hand sanitizer for times when soap and water aren't available.

5. **Safe Food and Water**
Consume bottled water or boil tap water before drinking. Be cautious when eating street food and opt for well-cooked, hot meals.

6. **Sun Protection**
Wear sunscreen with a high SPF to protect your skin from the sun's rays. Also, wear hats, sunglasses, and protective clothing.

7. **Emergency Contact Information**
Keep a list of emergency contact numbers, including local emergency services, your country's embassy or consulate, and your travel insurance provider.

8. **Local Laws and Customs**
Familiarize yourself with local laws and customs to avoid unintentional offenses. Respect cultural norms and dress codes.

9. **Stay Hydrated**
Carry a reusable water bottle and drink plenty of water, especially if you're engaging in outdoor activities.

10. **Safe Transportation**
Use reputable transportation services and adhere to seatbelt and helmet regulations. Be cautious when crossing streets, especially in busy areas.

11. **Travel with a Companion**
- Whenever possible, explore the area with a companion, especially during nighttime outings.

12. **Secure Valuables**
- Use hotel safes to store passports, extra money, and valuable items. Keep a photocopy of important documents.

13. **Stay Informed**
- Stay updated on local news and any travel advisories that may affect your trip.

CHAPTER 8: Beyond Le Havre: Exploring Normandy

Day Trips to Nearby Towns and Villages

Exploring the charming towns and villages surrounding Le Havre in Normandy is a delightful way to experience the region's diversity. Here are some day trip options to consider:

1. **Honfleur**
Known for its picturesque harbor, colorful buildings, and art galleries, Honfleur offers a relaxed atmosphere and maritime charm.

2. **Étretat**
Famous for its dramatic cliffs, natural arches, and stunning coastal views, Étretat is a paradise for nature lovers and hikers.

3. **Deauville**
A glamorous seaside resort known for its upscale boutiques, elegant promenade, and beautiful sandy beach.

4. **Trouville-sur-Mer**
Adjacent to Deauville, Trouville-sur-Mer features a charming fishing port, seafood restaurants, and a lively fish market.

5. **Cabourg**
A charming seaside town with a long sandy beach, elegant architecture, and a lovely promenade.

6. **Bayeux**
Home to the famous Bayeux Tapestry, this historic town offers medieval streets, a beautiful cathedral, and informative museums.

7. **Caen**

A city with a rich history, including William the Conqueror's castle and the Memorial Museum dedicated to World War II.

8. **Giverny**

Visit Claude Monet's former home and garden, where you can stroll through the beautiful flower gardens that inspired his famous paintings.

9. **Rouen**

Explore the capital of Normandy, known for its stunning cathedral, medieval architecture, and Joan of Arc history.

10. **Mont-Saint-Michel**

- Although it's a bit further, Mont-Saint-Michel is worth a day trip for its iconic abbey perched on a rocky island and breathtaking surroundings.

Exploring the Normandy Countryside: Landmarks and Natural Beauty

Exploring the charming Normandy countryside from Le Havre offers a delightful escape into a realm of picturesque landscapes, historic landmarks, and serene beauty. Here's a guide to some of the must-visit landmarks and natural wonders that await you:

1. **Étretat Cliffs**: Just a short drive from Le Havre, the Étretat Cliffs are an iconic natural wonder. These dramatic limestone formations rise majestically from the sea, offering breathtaking views and opportunities for scenic hikes. The "Aiguille" and "Porte d'Aval" are among the most famous formations, each telling a story etched by the sea's embrace.

2. **Mont Saint-Michel**: While a bit farther from Le Havre, a visit to Mont Saint-Michel is a journey into medieval enchantment. This UNESCO World Heritage Site is a tidal island topped by a stunning abbey. As you explore its narrow streets and admire the architecture, you'll understand why it's often referred to as the "Wonder of the Western World."

3. **Honfleur**: This picturesque port town is a haven for artists and visitors alike. Stroll along the Vieux Bassin, the old harbor surrounded by colorful buildings, and admire the reflection of boats in the water. Honfleur's cobbled streets,

art galleries, and maritime ambiance create a captivating experience.

4. **Giverny**: Art and nature converge in Giverny, the home of renowned impressionist painter Claude Monet. Visit Monet's house and the famous water lily pond that inspired his masterpieces. The beautifully landscaped gardens, bursting with color and life, offer an immersive experience in Monet's creative world.

5. **Château de Chambord**: A longer day trip from Le Havre, Château de Chambord is a Renaissance masterpiece nestled in the Loire Valley. Its intricate architecture, grand halls, and expansive grounds invite you to step back in time and imagine the opulent lives of its former residents.

6. **D-Day Landing Beaches**: For history enthusiasts, a visit to the D-Day Landing Beaches is a poignant experience. These historic sites played a pivotal role in World War II and are now commemorated with museums, memorials, and preserved bunkers that offer a glimpse into the events of that era.

7. **Pays d'Auge**: Embark on a scenic drive through the picturesque Pays d'Auge region, famous for its charming villages, rolling hills, and apple orchards. This area is renowned for producing delicious cider and Calvados, the apple brandy that is a signature of Normandy.

8. **Rouen**: This historic city is known for its stunning Gothic architecture, including the Rouen Cathedral, which inspired many of Monet's paintings. Explore its medieval streets, visit the Place du Vieux Marché where Joan of Arc was martyred, and indulge in its culinary delights.

9. **Suisse Normande:** The "Norman Switzerland" is a rugged area characterized by its deep valleys, rocky terrain, and winding rivers. Outdoor enthusiasts can engage in activities such as hiking, kayaking, and rock climbing while soaking in the natural beauty.

10. **Bayeux**: Home to the famous Bayeux Tapestry, which depicts the events leading up to the Norman Conquest of England, Bayeux offers a glimpse into medieval history. Explore

the tapestry, visit the Bayeux Cathedral, and stroll through the charming town.

As you venture beyond Le Havre into the Normandy countryside, you'll discover a tapestry of landscapes, history, and culture that enriches your travel experience. Each landmark and natural wonder tells a story, inviting you to connect with the region's past and present in profound ways.

Basic phrases

Greetings

Hello: Bonjour
Good evening: Bonsoir
Hi: Salut
Goodbye: Au revoir

Polite Expressions

Please: S'il vous plaît
Thank you: Merci
You're welcome: De rien
Excuse me / Sorry: Excusez-moi / Pardon

Introductions

My name is [Your Name]: Je m'appelle [Votre Nom]
What's your name?: Comment vous appelez-vous?
Nice to meet you: Enchanté(e)

Asking for Help

Can you help me?: Pouvez-vous m'aider?
I don't understand: Je ne comprends pas
Could you repeat that?: Pouvez-vous répéter?

Directions

Where is [Place]?: Où se trouve [Lieu]?
How do I get to [Place]?: Comment je vais à [Lieu]?
Left / Right: Gauche / Droite
Straight ahead: Tout droit

Ordering Food

I would like...: Je voudrais...
Menu, please: La carte, s'il vous plaît
Water: Eau

Check, please: L'addition, s'il vous plaît

Numbers

1: Un
2: Deux
3: Trois
4: Quatre
5: Cinq
6: Six
7: Sept
8: Huit
9: Neuf
10: Dix

Common Phrases

Yes: Oui
No: Non
I don't know: Je ne sais pas
How much is it?: Combien ça coûte?
Excuse me, where is the bathroom?: Excusez-moi, où sont les toilettes?

Making an effort to speak a few basic phrases in the local language can go a long way in showing respect and building connections with the people you meet in Le Havre. French locals will appreciate your attempts, even if your pronunciation isn't perfect!

CONCLUSION

It's a moment to reflect on the incredible experiences that have unfolded while exploring Le Havre. This city, with its unique blend of elegance, heritage, and adventure, offers a truly unforgettable experience.

From the very beginning, Le Havre's coastal charm draws you in. The soothing sounds of the waves, the gentle sea breeze, and the sight of boats bobbing in the harbor leave an indelible mark on your heart. As you walk through the streets, you witness a city that has risen from the ashes with an incredible spirit of resilience and innovation.

The journey takes you through the world of art and culture, from the magnificent works at the MuMa to the awe-inspiring architecture that defines the city's skyline. The beaches provide moments of serenity and reflection, while the nearby cliffs of Étretat take you on a journey through time and nature's wonders.

And let's not forget the culinary delights that Le Havre has to offer. Exploring the local markets, indulging in the flavors of Normandy's cuisine, and sharing meals with friends and fellow travelers add a delicious layer to your adventure.

As you venture beyond Le Havre's borders, you discover the treasures of the Normandy countryside—historic landmarks, charming villages, and breathtaking landscapes that deepen your connection to this region.

And now, as we prepare to say goodbye to Le Havre, it's a moment to express gratitude for sharing this journey. The memories created, the connections made, and the stories collected will remain with you, reminding you of the beauty and richness that this city has to offer. So, as you close this chapter, carry the spirit of Le Havre with you, knowing that its elegance, heritage, and adventure will always have a place in your heart. Until you meet again on new adventures, take care and bon voyage.

BONUS: Travel Journal

TRAVEL Itinerary Planner

Date:

Flight number:

Hotel number:

ITEMS TO BRING

PLACES TO VISIT

NOTES

Activity:

Budget:

Food:

TRAVEL Itinerary Planner

Date:

Flight number:

Hotel number:

ITEMS TO BRING

PLACES TO VISIT

NOTES

Activity:

Budget:

Food:

TRAVEL Itinerary Planner

Date:

Flight number:

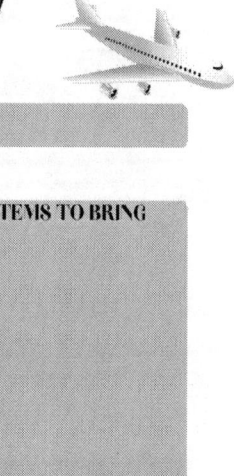

ITEMS TO BRING

Hotel number:

PLACES TO VISIT

NOTES

Activity:

Budget:

Food:

TRAVEL Itinerary Planner

Date:

Flight number:

ITEMS TO BRING

Hotel number:

PLACES TO VISIT

NOTES

Activity:

Budget:

Food:

TRAVEL Itinerary Planner

Date:

Flight number:

ITEMS TO BRING

Hotel number:

PLACES TO VISIT

NOTES

Activity:

Budget:

Food:

TRAVEL Itinerary Planner

Date:

Flight number:

Hotel number:

ITEMS TO BRING

PLACES TO VISIT

NOTES

Activity:

Budget:

Food:

TRAVEL Itinerary Planner

Date:

Flight number:

ITEMS TO BRING

Hotel number:

PLACES TO VISIT

NOTES

Activity:

Budget:

Food:

TRAVEL Itinerary Planner

Date:

Flight number:

ITEMS TO BRING

Hotel number:

PLACES TO VISIT

NOTES

Activity:

Budget:

Food:

TRAVEL Itinerary Planner

Date:

Flight number:

ITEMS TO BRING

Hotel number:

PLACES TO VISIT

NOTES

Activity:

Budget:

Food:

TRAVEL Itinerary Planner

Date:

Flight number:

ITEMS TO BRING

Hotel number:

PLACES TO VISIT

NOTES

Activity:

Budget:

Food:

TRAVEL Itinerary Planner

Date:

Flight number:

Hotel number:

PLACES TO VISIT

ITEMS TO BRING

NOTES

Activity:

Budget:

Food:

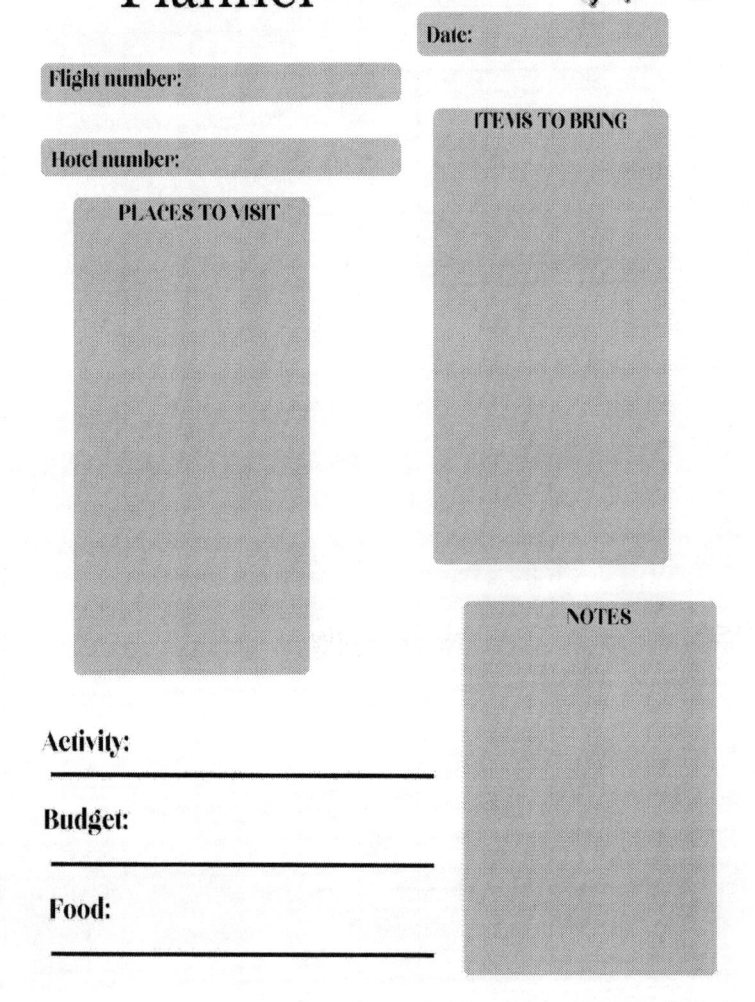

TRAVEL Itinerary Planner

Date:

Flight number:

Hotel number:

ITEMS TO BRING

PLACES TO VISIT

NOTES

Activity:

Budget:

Food:

TRAVEL Itinerary Planner

Date:

Flight number:

ITEMS TO BRING

Hotel number:

PLACES TO VISIT

NOTES

Activity:

Budget:

Food:

TRAVEL Itinerary Planner

Date:

Flight number:

Hotel number:

ITEMS TO BRING

PLACES TO VISIT

NOTES

Activity:

Budget:

Food:

TRAVEL Itinerary Planner

Date:

Flight number:

ITEMS TO BRING

Hotel number:

PLACES TO VISIT

NOTES

Activity: _____

Budget: _____

Food: _____

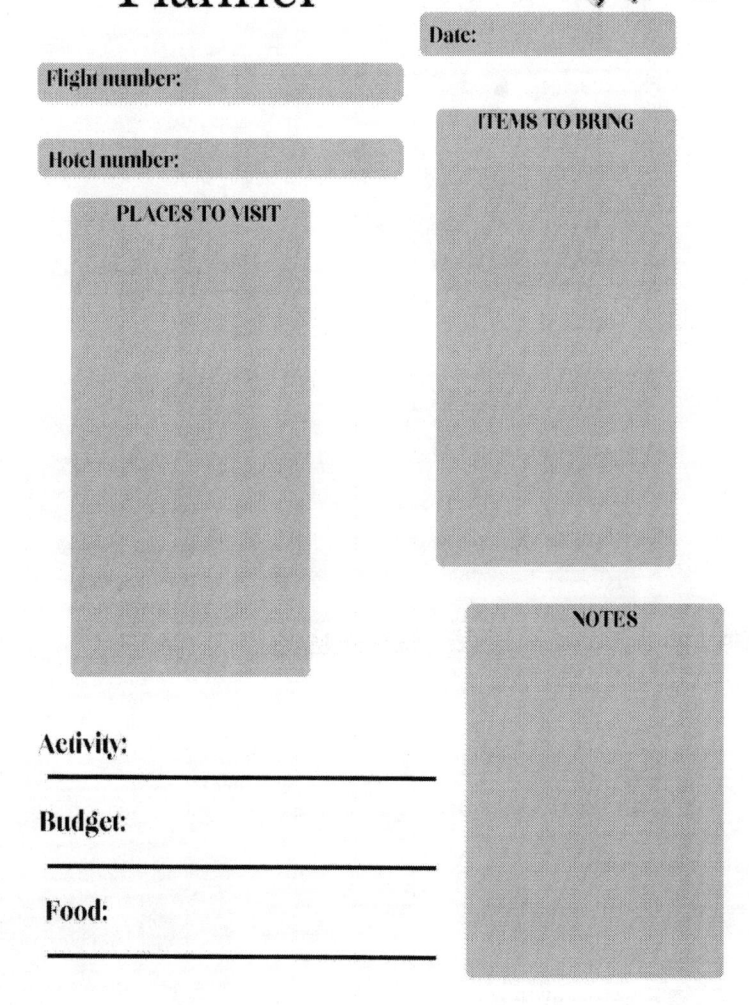

TRAVEL Itinerary Planner

Date:

Flight number:

ITEMS TO BRING

Hotel number:

PLACES TO VISIT

NOTES

Activity:

Budget:

Food:

TRAVEL Itinerary Planner

Date:

Flight number:

ITEMS TO BRING

Hotel number:

PLACES TO VISIT

NOTES

Activity:

Budget:

Food:

TRAVEL Itinerary Planner

Date:

Flight number:

Hotel number:

ITEMS TO BRING

PLACES TO VISIT

NOTES

Activity:

Budget:

Food:

TRAVEL Itinerary Planner

Date:

Flight number:

Hotel number:

ITEMS TO BRING

PLACES TO VISIT

NOTES

Activity:

Budget:

Food:

TRAVEL Itinerary Planner

Date:

Flight number:

Hotel number:

ITEMS TO BRING

PLACES TO VISIT

NOTES

Activity:

Budget:

Food:

Made in United States
Orlando, FL
25 February 2024